To Purple

Happy Birthday

COMING HOME

love

Nigel

*'Last night I saw the angels beat at the door of the tavern,
The clay of Adam they shaped, and into the mould they cast'*

Hafiz (1320-90)

───────────── Acknowledgements ─────────────

Tom and Dorothy Hopkinson
whose idea it was;

Bhau Kalchuri, consultant
on the ghazals;

the King of Hearts;

Several of these poems have
been previously published
in 'Anglo Welsh Review',
'Creative Language',
'Schools' Poetry Review'
Delhi London Poetry Quarterly'
and 'Encounter'

ISBN 0 9518657 0 6
Coming Home (Pbk)
1st Edition

Design, typesetting and cover illustration
by Marion Catlin

Set in Perpetua throughout
Printed on Solaire paper kindly supplied by
Robert Horne Paper Company Ltd
Printed in England by Rigby Print, Norwich

— *for Melanie* —

This book is about a journey, and it started as a personal one for its author, which took him seven years. Soon after the work was completed, I invited Gareth to read a selection of the poems at the King of Hearts, a centre for people and the arts in Norwich. It then became a personal adventure for me, as the impact of the reading made me feel that here was a work worthy of publication: not only did the poet have something of significance to say, he also had the words to say it, so that the content was perfectly served by the form - a balance not often found.

The purpose is ambitious: to address the age old questions "Who am I? Where do I come from? Where am I going?" It is a perilous task to attempt the setting of this huge theme in poetic form. The risk of being pedantic, heavy, or esoteric, is present at every turn of the road. Even an inspired writer like Victor Hugo, who had a similar purpose in parts of "Les Contemplations" and "La Légende des Siècles", did not avoid those pitfalls, and the result is an avalanche of metaphors which goes on for thousands of verses.

Fortunately for his readers, Gareth Calway belongs to the classical approach, described by André Gide as "the art of saying less in order to express more". Neither didactic nor obscure, his style is sharp without being dry, leaving space for things unsaid and the reader's own experience. He uses a wide variety of poetic forms, from the villanelle, the ballad and the sonnet through to the Persian ghazal. The discipline of structure is never a formalistic exercise, but a way to channel and express the feeling, mood or meaning. Each poem can stand on his own, a glimpse of a moment in time, a facet of experience. However, the work's impact is in the whole, which is the account of a momentous journey: the journey of the soul towards its home, its perfection. Starting with the unformed state of gas and stardust, the soul then cloaks itself in all the successive forms of creation from stone to leaf, to animal, culminating in the human form ("Evolution"). As humans, we then struggle through the ups and downs of history, caught in the suffering and the hope for a better world ("Ghosts"); until eventually there comes the realisation that home is not of this world, and that the key to it all is love ("Involution") .

The brief explanatory passages which precede each section were written for the public reading, and have been kept, at my request, in order to help the understanding of the whole. I am not of the school which relishes mystery at the expense of clarity, and I welcome the poet extending a helping hand to his readers.

It is now your turn, Reader, to embark on the journey: bon voyage, and may you arrive home in your own good time!

Aude Gotto
Director of the King of Hearts

CONTENTS

I. EVOLUTION

II. GHOSTS

CONTENTS

III. INVOLUTION

I. EVOLUTION

Evolution is about the constituents of human experience and consciousness inherited from the process of evolution (animal, vegetable and mineral). It explores the notion that we retain gas-consciousness, stone-consciousness, metal-consciousness, vegetation-consciousness, fish-consciousness, bird-consciousness and animal-consciousness in us and that these need to be fully worked out and experienced before we can become fully human. For example, when confronted by someone in tears, our reaction might be to take refuge in a cold impersonality summed up in the popular phrase 'heart of stone'.When seriously threatened we might bark, snarl and grimace like a dog, though we do so using human language and means. We deny in effect the very existence of an other who challenges our exclusive sense of reality. Other popular phrases sum up these pre-human strategies with uncanny insight. A human 'creep' subsists on the spineless techniques perfected by the worm; a 'snake in the grass' adds to this the cunning viciousness of a reptile. This is quite acceptable, indeed laudable, in a reptile but appallingly reductive in a human being which has infinitely finer potential (the potential explored in 'Involution'). 'Randy as a bull' refers to sub-human human sexuality and there are countless other such phrases used to describe, in humans, a reproductive vigour and stamina more proper to animals. The evolutionary process is not, though, a negative one. While the other poems are about the individual stages being worked through, the first poem views Evolution as a positive whole. Poetry is acknowledged as an inspirational striving towards the fully human, like all art, at the end of this first poem.

As consciousness evolves, it is manifested in higher and higher forms. The poetic form chosen in each case attempts to reflect this: gas as 'formless' verse; stone as a claustrophobic villanelle; vegetation as free verse, though restricted in comparison to the wide-ranging verse-freedom of 'Animal', and so on. The perfect - human - form is expressed as an irregular Petrarchan sonnet, (the form to suggest the unique human capacity for conscious control; the irregularity to suggest each human's individuality and freedom). This - the only fully upright form -, though made up of stone (bones, minerals), vegetable growth (hair, nails) and all the lower forms up to and including the higher animals, both subsumes and transcends them all, as well as containing within it all the aspirations of the human spirit. The pre-human forms which cramp and de-humanise are, at the same time, the very stuff out of which human potential is created. The miracle of this seems to demand religious language.

The giggle of gas.
The stability of stone.
The mildness and might of metal.
The vigour of vegetation.
The wiliness of the worm,
Out of its depth.
The flowing finesse of a fish
Out of water, beating its scales
Into hard-won wings.
The balance of bird
At height of career,
Still finding its feet.
The power and the glory
Of the she-tiger
In the cat upon the lap,
Thrust from its napping.
The sum of all these
And their greater whole
In human being.
But the growing
Consciousness that each
Is a drop in the ocean
Compared with the love
That drowns life and death.

Of these, Muse Beloved, for You,
I sing.

Before there was light,
In a coma, darkly,
Before there was dark,
I was One,
All-Unknowing
But now I'm uncentred
Energy - None - ,
A frozen fart
Glowing round in circles
All over place
Marking time.
If you look for a heart.
You'll find

ice

ammonia

methane

vapour

space-waste

dust.

Nothing of substance.

Look for identity,
You'll find it unfixed
In a skin of gases
Blowing hot and cold,
In features of dust
Following wherever
The solar wind blows,
I have no principle
Of integration,
Except at most
A coldly unmoved
Diffusing together
Of everything and nothing;
Nor is my retrograde
Orbit of Sun
A wish for a centre.
Sun is my enemy.
Each time we meet,
I lose myself,
Lose face in His dazzle,
Lose head in His blast,
Tail off in a million
Gas-sweating miles
Dust into dust.

Nor do I need Him
(That my brilliance is mostly

His, reflected
I icily deny).
I am luminous, head
As big as a planet
And unusually bright,
I've been around;

Seen the birth of Light
Shining in the darkness,
Comprehended it not;
Watched Empires tremble,
Nations falling,
Maintained my course;
Take everything in,
Give nothing away.

All this hot air
All this snowballing flash
Sperming its two-tailed way
Down the void
Preserves on ice

My tiny secret.

A core of regret
(Cloudily whispered)

The seed of a heart.

Almighty, endless, metamorphosis!
Birth of the deadliest thing on the planet,
The Verb into noun, the process into stasis.

Damn all these currents of feeling that kiss
And wear me, so much, with their wetness, or grit,
Almighty, endless, metamorphosis.

Sunshine, tears, won't melt my heart like Ice's,
I'm dead hard. Whatever moves, I'll kill it,
The Verb into noun, the process into stasis.

Silence; a stare: are my anaesthetists.
I freeze out pressure, heat. I won't admit
Almighty, endless, metamorphosis.

I went to pieces once; perhaps round this
More grainy core, less brittle, I can fit
The Verb into noun, the process into stasis.

Made of dead reactions, buried stresses,
Grist to milling Earth, I'll never quit
Almighty, endless, metamorphosis,
The Verb into noun, the process into stasis.

for two voices

He: It's very dark in here. I'm paralysed,
Dormant and dreamless. Feel poles
Of heat and cold, unchanged. And neutralise

Them. Don't know what to do with myself, doled
With endless wastes of time to kill. Waiting
For someone to turn me up, an end to hold

Onto. Feel a distant purity but ring
False, hopelessly flawed and dull, when struck. Dumb.
Things happen *to* me. Especially nothing.

I spent a short time somewhere crowded, numb.
About eight million years. There was lots
Of immigrant stuff I'd (vaguely) become

A part of. It was probably chaos.
I just lay back, let it all not happen.
Then there was a change. The night was a-buzz,

Vibrating. And I - it was quite sudden
I suppose - was in two places at once.
It got - warmer. My molecules loosened,

Got a little excited.... Ages thence,
It registered that the immigrant stuff,
With impossible speed, had vanished, whence

I was more my own thing. Though a good half
(In two different places) was missing,
Cut. - But that's neither here nor there. I have

No lost identity. I feel nothing.

She: Can't move. Can't. Move. Can only steel my grain
           Against him, against more change. Petrified.
           - And why should I? Nothing ever mends. I'm

           Stuck with myself, though God alone knows why.
           I never asked to be here. Molten Light's
           Delirium conceived me just to lie

           Beneath the piled milleniums of Night
           In everlasting restlessness. I'd been
           Going nowhere. Slowly. Coldly. My bright

           Beginning finished soon as it began.
           Now I'm in my own way. Too dense to shift
           From it. In a life without end.... I'm dammed.

           The only chance I've got - of real Life -
           Is being overcome by Force. Another's.
           But afterwards I'd only lie there. Stiff,

           As if unmoved. Regardless. Why bother?

He: I want her but won't give a mile, an inch.
           She's only a bit of stuff. But, oh, she's
           Heaven. If only she'd yield, I'd be so rich!

She: I've done with cast-offs, drossy jewels and quartz.
           I was bathed in cyanide to free me,
           Though a false gleam conceals it, of course.

           I hate and despise, like poison, sweety,
           These clods, detest their coarsened common feel.
           I'm *refined* (if you even know what it means).

           No. Not just 'polished' my so-called 'dear'. *Real.*

He: You needed nerves of steel just to survive
        Where I came from. You were given a scrape
        And crushed from the start. Bent. All your insides

        Exposed. Filed. Drilled into shape.
        You needed a tempered will like iron,
        Smoothness and flash a hammer couldn't break.

        The fault's my background. Not whom it picked on.

She: You want me? Why? Does a certain stable
        Fluency attract you to me, blending
        My lightness and grace? I'm pliable

        If you really try. But I risk nothing,
        It's just how I am, it doesn't move me.
        To you it's magnetic. All this straining

        To reach me's *your* problem. *Your* star. (Icy).

He: I feel half-dead. My other half's somewhere
        Else. One day I'll be got back in one piece,
        Perhaps. Meanwhile, I've been jolted half-aware

        In opposite directions. Once.... Or twice....

She: Or not.... No amount of chemistry,
        No amount of warmth, no amount of time
        Can touch me. Put your life's current through me

        I'll stay switched off. Like lead, for all my shine.

He: I can't wake up. Such fatigue! It's so hard
        To push through this irresistible dark, Fate's
        Immoveable object - myself....I'm shattered.

Only once, I was dreaming of a shape
Brilliantly mettled, Primely Moving. It all
Came together, in every place....

She.   Oh yes, I've dreamt of a true Golden Age
Where I, the immutable Iron Maid,
Break out at last of that golden cage,

Dim memory melting riveted gaze,
Endure, am accepted in, a world I embrace.
Touch. Know - another being. Feel ....

Escape....

                But - No. I'm too rusted in place
In my rustlessness. I will play it straight.
Keep a grip. Lie low. Remain poker-faced.

Preserve my goodness, value, glow.   And wait.

Puckered,
Naked,
Grizzly,
Clenched,
Ugly as a newborn face;
Scared to let myself go:
And where can I go
Except towards death?
And what if I grow
In the wrong directions,
Abnormal or twisted,
And how do you do it anyway?
Thoughts crumpled,
Feelings crushed,
Perhaps I'm not even a leaf,
Just scared to stand out
From the crowded branches?
So what am I? - yellow?
Or just painfully shy
Soft virgin green,
Closed against the urging sun?
Do I have to do anything?
Will I just become - me?
Or do I have to force myself out?
Safer to sit tight;
But then I get scared
The rest of the branch
Which had seemed so wooden
Is unfolding faster;
Best to let go, then;
But what if my flower
Hardly out of bud
Gets pollinated?

The May blossom light
Of the still warm evening:
The birdsong high
Above distant traffic:
God become mild
And expansive, beaming:
The breathless wind:
All give their answer:
He who saves his dances
Will never be a dancer.

i'm a creep,
a real crawler,
no backbone
at all, a

low, humble
grinder, base
mouth full
of soil, a

wet, writhing
hyper-
sensed slave
to all, a

chill, faceless
horror, tightlipped,
toothless
scrawl, a

dim, brainless
shrinker from
harm, a cringing
coil, but a -

live!
     and i can turn

To a snake in the grass, or in your bosom,
(Or under a garland of bright apple blossom),
Moving you deep in your bowels:
Subtly developed, sophisticated,
Staring through hooded, lidless eyes
At a dense underworld, dimmed, deaf as Dis,
Feeling my sniff-flicking way with my tongue,
With a wriggle of ribs, swift-scaling the dust,
Dumb, unless rattled, when, breath caught, I hiss.

I'm
Puffed up with sluggish irritation,
Stitched in a dead skin, a splintered vision,
Excreted through rocks like fear, or birth,
Charmed by your writhing arms, scared of sticks,
The dinosaur undead, too potent to handle,
Daemonic, divine, river written in the stars,
Smooth poison keeping Creation sweet,
The dragon. Get off my back or I'll strike you.

You've wanted me always, under your heel.

You cleared off
Into Upper Space,
Taking your first small giant steps
Into the Primaeval Future
While I stayed,

Coral-jointed a cage
Of nerve-threaded bone,
Fleshing it out with rippling muscle,
Knotting together the deep, welling ages
Of fright and flight,

A twitch of my streamlined wings
Keeping me safe,

Shaping up
In the queerest ways
To the all-consuming challenge,
The whelming, drowning influence
Of Cold Water,

Coming out of my shell
To conquer the world
With love-'n'-warpaint, guts and chainmail,
A show of backbone,
A gritting of teeth

And this rigid fanatic's stare
That never looks forward to anything

Else; head never raised
(Unless I should get
A half-frigid mouth
Hooked on your faithful, singing line)
From a shoalful of furies,

Fears, flirtations,
Fatherly flutters,
A fishy identification with place,
A thirst like an Ocean
I'll never drown:

The unblinking dreams
Of an outgrown brain.

Somewhere beyond those pitching treetops
And dizzy roofs and towers,
Distant mountains and wild blue seas,
In a heaven of grub and flowers
Is home. But these eyes won't spy it.
Though I've brooded on wingspan, wind and waves,
Density, distance, directions,
Hoarded and waited, cracked tiny brains
On pressure gauge, plotting and preparations,
I still haven't learned how to fly.

Breezily gullible, I'd always believed
It would flow as freely as my fantasies:
Heroic escape into pure, hawkish heights,
Soft-hearted lovey-dovey airs, mercy flights,
An enriching, elevating experience, they said,
Be upright, self-supporting, lofty....and dead.

Edge of the nest. In a flap. (Afraid).
But had to escape from Mother.
Squawk squawk squawk. No room. Need air.
Then - Mummy, it's giddy up here.
My heart flutters, sinks - lacking dawn to lift
My petrified beak in a song-throat's soaring.
I'm sorry I ruffled your feathers, Mum.
Please take me back under your wing.

Sun breaks in. "Rise up. Follow me.
Don't freeze for a moment to think of The Fall,
That you're wing-clipped, that really there is No Way;
That miles from Nowhere Else, alone,
You'll end as some ground-snaking Evil's prey;
Take it. Before your brain even twigs.
That leap in the dark of faith, or death,
That flight from your nestling worm of doubt,
Into this screaming cloud of breath."

An An An An
Ger. Ger.
Lost
Miles from homeground
And every outpost
But Keep Off. Off.
I defend.
An An An
Therefore (for the moment)
I am.

Running
Wild and lone and free
Yet wanting
To run with the pack
And howl with the pack
And fight for my place
(I'm a social animal).
A single life
Is like digging for Nothing
Or barking up the wrong tree.
An An An An

Ger.
To be brutally honest,
For all its trails
Of blazing fragrance,
When you look at it
Life is grey.
But then every Now
Now Now Now Now, there's this
White
And, still,
White
Fire in the sky

And it makes no sense
It being there
And it makes me feel
So lonesome and lowdown and far away.
Ow. Howl.
And I can't comprehend it.
Not even with teeth that can take things apart
(And might just start with your face.)

Rationalised vertebrae,
Far more competitive
Than the reptile model.
Elastic skin for a robe of hair.
Nerve.
High-centred brainwaves.
A programmed delay
In the struggle for survival
For reason to grow.
(A suck like the void).
A warm heart. A deep breath.
Such is the mould
Of my restlessness,
My hunger and drive,
My endless animation,
My sleep full of whimpers and sighing,
My animal jive. It's
An ark full of animus
And joy. Animal fierce and animal
Peaceful: catty bloodthirsty self-sufficient
Vertical sabre-tooth jawed; bovine
Long-winded grinding-everything-sideways
Over-and-over-again cowed. The scampering
Hunted; the lumbering secure (animal
Successful). The graceful, long, rapid
Striding chasers; the short, slow

Food-bolting flee-ers (animal graceless).
The burrowers-out-of-the-ratrace
Failures; the climbers-out-of-the-ratrace
Successes. The sleek 'A' stream swimmers;
The webbed-hand low fliers. Basic design:
To lift the body high above creeping ground
But not the eye. Grand alimentary canals
Leading gloriously up their own backsides.

Miles from homeground
Chasing my tail.
Ow. Howl.
Never so foxed
Since I fled the Old Dog's
Paw on my back
For a pack of my own.
My drooping head
Guided by instinct
Gnawed sharper than plant,
Worm, fish or bird,
Doggedly pursues
The fading scent
Of self-preservation,
Stale routine
Of vomit retrieval,
Security-drops,
Stench of bitch,
Whiff of war, until
Lifted up,
Wordless ears pricking,
Great heart beaten,
Can't run any more,

By a voice I remember -
Master, calling.

for my daughter

My snow soul is slowly taking shape,
Falling from heaven to inherit the earth
And the family features of God and ape,
Angel out of my element from birth....
And this is me, this helpless drop of Man,
This perfect mould of bud and mineral,
Crawling, fight, and every earthly thing.
All of it - nothing.
                Yet I'll assert I AM
In time by striving upright endlessly;
Inherit here a kiss - to milk, like grist,
The love that made me and by which I'm born;
The word that speaks its perfect mind; the fist
That grasps its imaged God; the whole torn
And bleeding womb of human history.

GHOSTS

Having achieved human form, man makes history and is
made by it. 'Ghosts' is about this new habitat. Western
thought, since the Greeks and then the Renaissance, has
typically traced a logical progression, a growing and
purposive mastery of human and technological capabilities,
in this developing habitat. But its religions, derived from
the ('Near') East, identify the ultimate purpose of
existence as love and the search for God, a timeless
experience outside of and indifferent to history. Those
Eastern religions which, unlike Islam and Christianity, have
not been powerfully influenced by the West, go further, in
identifying continuous and purposive reincarnation as a
basic element in this search. These very different outlooks
are explored simultaneously in 'Ghosts': historically
generated people dialectically engaging with the possibilities
of each progressive age, on the one hand; souls - perhaps
even the same soul - engaged with the material world but
longing for something beyond it, on the other ('Involution'
pursues this further). But the two outlooks are not, apart
from the idea of reincarnation, mutually exclusive. Indeed
they are not really separable.

The form chosen is typical of the speaker's specific
historical habitat in each case. Gwenefore is a dark age
Briton; Lady Guinevere a mediaeval Norman (the
Arthurian legend links two distinct cultures and eras).
'539' is the authenticated date of a mutually ruinous
British civil war which climaxed at Camlann. "Ravens will
flock on the gore" adapts from the Welsh a line in an
ancient battle poem. "The wolves' dread evensong"
borrows the metaphor of an eighth century monk. The
syllabic form of "Jewess" is that of Job's Outburst in the
Revised Standard Version of the Bible. The Bristol sections
recount events witnessed by my family. The rest - a
reconstruction from primary texts - is history.

Strophe

What is history? Hector's gone.
Opposites create, but not for long.
Loser makes winner, winner takes all,
Hybris gallops before a fall.
The history-makers have a day at best
Then history marches into The West.
Whence have we come? where do we go?
Until we come there, how can we know?
The hero is tragic, the unborn best
And time flies on and finds no rest.
Though god-armed Achilles won the war,
The heel is sand that bruised the shore.
Life's certain as crowd-pulling Icarus.
Strife's the father of all. And all's flux....

Anti-strophe

The gods are dead: our explanation
Of World must come from sense-perception.
Science and reason teach self-control:
Body's the tomb, the prison, of soul.
Mathematical meditation
Frees the psyche of incarnation.
Nothing changes: God is reason
And His nous the only action.
Pleasure's merely pain deferred:
Virtue is its own reward.
Though Socrates for wisdom dies,
Nothing born of woman thrives.
The world of ideas alone is real,
Beyond emotion and time - Ideal.

Epode

Then muse upon the Perfect Man,
The Heracles of Bethlehem,
Who was before the world began
And will be when it finds its end;
ioropia, conceived in Greece,
Is wed to Love (which razes mind)
Made breathless and beyond decease
By nine scored months of Roman time;
Our cradle of democracy
Is stalled with beasts and barboroi,
Our tragedy and comedy -
The kristos in a craftsman's boy;
And hunt through time a timeless quest,
Making history, going West....

ioropia: (Gr.) history

Antonius to Epimachus, his father and lord, many greetings.

thanks for your lines which were sent in the summer and
found me today. it's like the end of the world out here!
still it's promotion, and things were getting
over hot in the Province by the time I left.
too many raving messiahs with swords.
well. i've borne blood and terror out East for too long,
I hope these 'Iceni' see the benefits of Rome
with rather less persuasion.
and grant us, Mithras,
a governor who makes a few less mistakes.

Nazarenes preaching in Rome, you complain.
that's an amazing coincidence.
he was the one I told you about
crucified on one of my duties
(called in from Syria, as usual, for Troubles
too tricky for local auxilliaries) and
truly, he died like the son of a god. I was
so busy thinking of my new post and
reputation, and how to impose it on the crowd,
I didn't have time to notice much, just
managed an ambiguous, crowd-pleasing
gesture: a sponge of vinegar wine.
gods, and I hope that it helped him.
something about him's still making me restless.
I was glad to get out of that hot
stew of fanaticism at any rate....an old
Greek city would have done as well, but out west in the
wilds you get right away

from that gaze of astonishing beauty and sadness,
ah, as if dead, before death, and yet *so* alive with
'love', I was going to say: Hebrew hysteria
touch of that flaming provincial sun.

what is love?
in the real world, father (the world of Rome),
love is a wrestle between men and girls,
gods are imperial power and fate.
only the jews could *love* a god

yet only the jews could hand one over to
soldiers, like these of mine here, for
dressing up as a comedy king, in a
flesh and blood tragedy; soldiers as
hard as the nails that they drove through his hands, through
                    his twitching hands, and then
screams, and they diced for his robes as if robes were the
                    pearls, the swine, and you'll
call me mad, but I do
laud this humiliorus - this jew - I raised no finger to save,
I thrice promoted for saving the day (one day) for
Rome, somewhere. in his eyes I seemed to see
cracks in the roads we haven't even built
sprouting grass; Roman nettles and roses gone wild
reclaiming the forums, basilicae and temples:
Great Rome, itself, gods forbid, vandalised. these
tribesmen here with their longhaired resistance,
shapeless, impractical, formless lives,
ferocious druid charges, merely confirm us:
law, justice, trade, drains and good roads. it's as if
he will use us for a jewish
dream: dove descending on eagle, not eagle on
dove, humiliores inheriting the earth;
use us and then, maybe, throw all away like
chaff to barbarians in scattered hovels, - as if
Rome (not he, after all) were the dream.

but I'm wandering away from important matters.

here the new fortress expands by the hour. we at last have
a theatre.
still there's much more to square up, plant and build, before
I and, perhaps, my legion move on, leaving
peace and cultivation behind....this
Boudicca's causing a stir. have you heard of her?

orders are through. we must march. so in haste -

hail Caesar. vale.

A young Angle on night-watch.
The fire goes out.

the fire's flames flee   from dark's dagger drawn,
trees' twigs tremble,   my blood runs cold,
death-dread from deeps   from hills, from hollows,
through night-silence numbs   my axe-aching arms....
now darky-feet drumming   sheep-feet, horse-feet,
wolf-howl, bear-roar,   rain-start and rain-stop;
today's crop of slaves   stir by my lord's boat,
the half-clearing crowds   with ghosts from bad dreams;
no light now but starlight   fierce as gods' faces
to kindle my blood   or make sure my sight:
a witch of a watch   slumped in snake-fern
and no song of heroes   to cheer my chilled cheeks.
when I boast man's beard   I'll bear with my kin
the boat-gorging wave-road's   spite-spitting storms
and go from this fell ground   back to the fatherland.

Lord Arthur is gone, I laud my Beloved:
Cross on invincible shield, blood-red,
Dragon on young-summer green, red,
The terrible clatter of returning hooves.
I never quite believed. Always feared
Him dead. But he always came.

Arthur is gone, I laud my Beloved:
Swift white charger swooping like a spear
On the bonfire builders, the wolvers of women,
Scourging the rat-run inroads of Europe,
Animal tracks of attacking Saxon,
His spur-tensed Britons beat back the Beast.

Gone my Beloved, my Beloved I mourn:
Then Llugh fought battles within himself,
Cai fought his own rule, Bedwyr fought Llugh,
And some sought long for the holy caldron,
Sought it like a spoil of war,
And, gentle as light, my Beloved loved me.

And Medraut gnawed through the golden years
Myrddin called a threshold to the dark
And its beacon. Medraut, eyes on me
Like a dog's on the moon, snapping his moment.
To Camlann the coastland, carried me off.
Gone my Beloved, my Beloved I mourn.

And little the faith I had yet in Arthur,
The Angel campaigner, strong as light,
His sun-bright stars above the wicked forest
Seeming to fade. Rusty the scabbard,
Still magic the sword. And, once more, he came.
I've believed too little, I make my Confession.

At last I understood. The flincher from spears,
Medraut, was part of Arthur, his shadow,
Chancel and gargoyle had to be cancelled
Where all deeds are drowned, all swords returned:
Avalon. And I'll run no more.
I've believed too little, I make my Confession.

Night, and this nunnery, will fall. Ravens
Will flock on the gore. Let others keep
A glimmer, a glorious page, of Logres alight
Until the dawn. My Confession's done.
Still, my heart waits for hoofbeats.
(Still, my heart waits for hoofbeats....)

Lindisfarne. The Year of our Lord 792

The winter wind whines through the brittle trees,
Rattles the new glass,
The Celt-stone flags beat up their chill
Through my novice's sandals.

Gaudete! Gaudete! Christus est natus!

But the saint's tomb gives such an accession
Of incorruptible strength from within
That from prayer I rise without trouble,
Small wonder of many seen.

In nomine Patris, et Filii, et Spiritus Sancti.

From childhood I burned for a life religious;-
Child among devils and dirt,
Witch-fiends brewing the sea-chilled night,
The wolves' dread evensong.

Cum Sancto spiritu + in gloria Dei Patris.

  .... The miracle of Latin! its celestial music
  Rising like the arches of Rome,
  To my smoke-fevered eye, the ink angel-bright
  Cloistered from invasion of time....

My days filled now with candle and prayer,
Communal field-labour of love,
Christ's Mass held in common: a Nation, a family
Whose Father and blood-bond is God.

*Note: Lindisfarne was sacked in 793, marking the start of the
Viking raids on Britain.*

It was on a somer's evening
  The merry month of May,
When buds are free and briddës sing
  And leaves are brave and gay.

I met a surly Abbot
  Cruel steward at his side
And now his guards lay slain or fled
  But at me he did chide,

"Pawn so soiled and churlish,
  Living like a beast,
Your King crusades against the Turk,
  Spare me and join the feast."

"Norman," I laughed, "your danelaw's
  Ploughed every inch of this land,
You've snatched your danegeld twice and thrice
  With chainmail on your hand,

"Now stubborn as Danish sokeman
  And true as Saxon thegn
With a 'waes heal' and a freeman's shout
  We snatch it back again

"In the name of good King Alfred
  And the Nation that he saved,
In the Lincoln green of an English knight,
  We make our own Crusade.

"There's knight's blood on my longstaff
Fresh as the day I fled:
I hit him and hit him and hit him
And hit him until he was dead

"I'm much too far gone, Abbot,
For you to save my soul,
Besides, in that great pile of flesh,
Where's yours ? the devil's hole.

"For all your noble Churches
With turrets and with towers,
For all your royal forest laws
This venison is ours.

"Call for 'beef' and 'mutton',
It tastes like sheep and cow,
Stuff your pork till you're blue in the face,
It's villeins' pig and sow.

"You can keep your cuckoo's feathers,
Your fancy foreign drawl,
All we want back is the silver and gold
You loot by Cross and Law.

In the name of good King Alfred
And the Nation that he saved,
In the Lincoln green of an English knight,
We make our own Crusade."

Then swift as the sunlight's flicker
Behind the still-leafed tree,
I caught the chink of a tinkling spur
And a mounted lady's plea,

"Stout yeman, I beg your mercy
  Upon yon Abbot's life."
Golden hair flowed from her golden crown,
  In my heart went a long cool knife.

She'd never meant to parley
  Though she used the English tongue,
"You slew a knight whose daughter I am.
  Now your bowstring music's sung."

I planted my last arrow
  Deep in the forest green,
"Where it lands I live an outlaw forever."
  I fell at the feet of my Queen.

Now the light is painfully fading
  On the merry songs we sang
And the flight for our lives through the trees
  And the future left to hang....

In the name of God's King Alfred
  And the harvest that he saved,
Against these King-of-the-Castle knights,
  I've made my last Crusade.

Belle ami, si est de nous, Ne vous sans moi, ni moi sans vous.

Let them play at boyish games round
A table. Though walled up, bound,
In an unpublished garden, stone
Tower with window, all alone,
This court still revolves around *me*.
I twist them all round my pretty
Little finger, a studded ring:
The champion Knight, the poor King,
Modred, Gawain, my Lancelot.
It's the only power I know.
He comes through enchanted forests,
Rough-horses, haunted castles, mists;
From slaying Giants, big bad Knights,
Barons with feudal appetites;
Impossible quests for Our Lady,
Sowing wild seeds Love meant for me;
Obsessed so with courtly sin and
Confession - Indulgence's twin;
Greets Artos, old friend - clash of mail -
(So grieved his Crown still lacks a Graal),
So tedious! He comes to *me*
Who waits .... and do not wait to see
The object of his worship pass,
Wasted, into this looking glass,
Wheat-hair, rose-lips, unsown, should he
Choose to deny himself - and me.
I have a heart, self-determined,
Core of I Am, God-underpinned,
Won on the Cross, for me. It can
Choose a beloved, a 'husband'
The Church would make him. But marriage
On earth's not as it is - (a rich
Royal land transaction) as one
With my Lancelot - in heaven.

A Mystery Play

God on a church tower Cart, bearing an ark, against church wall.
Above cart, a shining stained-glass window (new).

GOD   The wick of Righteousness is low,
Man that I made, and rue, is My Foe,
Let rainfall lash, and tempests blow;
His fouled sky melt in the sea.

The chaos of Self-Seeking's clamour
Has drowned Love and Truth's hosanna,
But hark to My Thunder's hammer,
Drowned shall his Wilderness be.

He has poisoned my every command,
Waged wars in My Name, on My Land,
Let it blister, return to sand,
Greed's castles won't turn My Tide.

Yet, Noah, one forest conserve,
All creatures within it preserve
(Also thy wife) since My Laws ye serve,
My Children from Man's abuse hide.

NOAH   O Lord!....

Wife, dost thou list,World's belch in thine ear
Though whispered drops of Doom be here?
God's Chosen I am, to thee a mere
Drawer of stream water, waste.

Thou, mule of Eve, will not be ruled;
By Worldly Wisdom, Profit, schooled,
Thy hellsmouth-spitting, devil's fuel
Flies not this Flood. Make haste!

NOAH'S WIFE I'm damned if I'll cross an Ocean
Of God's Wrath on thy devotion
Of timber and forty odd nails. My potion
Is stronger, will help us to fly.

Live thou in the past. I'm not going.
Swill in this froth, it's all-knowing;
Our future is radiant and glowing;
Drink and be merry. Tomorrow we die....

The Year of our Lord 1605.

I am bringing the Word of God to His people.
They will hear God speaking through my English voice.
They will leave the gaudy tales of stained glass windows.
The picture books of children they shall put aside.
His glory shall sing in the chambers of their ears.
Long have I laboured in the lore of ancients:
God hath rewarded me with exceeding skill.
Pentecostal fire is under my tongue;
I am the instrument of Omnipotence
And all shall hear.
The mighty and proud with their 'gentil' Jesu
He shall bring down:
The mighty's "rex quondam, rexque futurus"
He shall bring down:
And the poor shall commit themselves unto thee;
Each Englishman's home shall be thy Castle,
A fortress for thy saints against the world:
We are building a new Jerusalem.

It will rise from the ruin of this stiff-necked realm.
Or, if rooted corruption revile thee again
As in former days
When English Bibles burned and their martyred makers,
Then boldly shall we sail into the Sun,
Ascend like wild geese into the whirlwind
And found His New World in a virgin land....
But first, I assert my rendering,
First, I must justify my lines before the Panel.
Surely my version rings truer than the others?

Surely it alone is authorised by God?
The scholar who precedes me is great indeed,
But listen to this, ye who have ears!....

....Yet, in my heart, I wonder much
If it liketh God
Or, indeed, if God liketh *me* at all.
I ought to be a purer vessel, yea a perfect man,
Ought not to be a man at all, but God.
All this cult of learning; this beautiful phrasing;
Is it merely a veil for my lack of love,
A disguise of my feeling nothing at all,
Not even doubt? Lord, I lack foundation.
Will thy mercy find me out?

Ah, humility.
I have stifled the breath of the Almighty.
John's line has it. His is truth. And it sings.
Mine is over-zealous for the form of the words -
I have missed their revelation.
But this line which follows,
There has truth found me,
Music, and majesty and moral in trinity,
Philosophy, figure and feeling in flight.
John and I, together, cement the Word,
All of us, together, cement the Word,
And the language of the Angles
And the language of the Angels
Shall be one.

(Culloden 1746)

So this is how it Ends, Silent and Slow,
Upended in these Marshes, Letting Go.
The Pain twists red but greys into the Sky
And soon will Fade, like Breath's Brief Mist, and Die.
The Way I'm fleeing no MacDonald harrows,
No Claymore in my Scarlet Target burrows.
I Retreat, without Regret, from this Life
Leaving Daughters, an Unprotected Wife,
A Mother - "Son, you're all I have," she said,
"It's hard to Let You Go," and still I'm Dead.
The April Blows hard, the hills stream with Song,
My gorsed Path keeps going, but I am Gone.
I fought for a Country, though not to stay
And maybe for Duke, but mostly for Pay;
The Ape who struck off my Name from the Roll
Does it for Clan-Chief and with his Whole Soul,
For Soil in which all his Tribe will be laid,
While I'll Enjoy a Private Grave.
Keen as Thistle, they hunt Us like Game
Then, drunk with Victory, go Home again;
Yet they Break the first Rule, cardinal Sin:
Never Give Combat Unless You Can Win.
And Die by One Law; One Protestant Line;
One Uniform Road to run Unchanging
Over my Body, through Heather and Fens,
Prehistoric Stones and Scotch-misted Glens
And all Ancient Haunts of kilted Clansmen:
A Race gone West, and my Spirit with them.

Wherever you go, it's still you,
The wind maun blaw the same.
This Scottish moon must mourn my bones,
Her nightingale my name.

A Vision

It is time we were making history,
This moment's immortal and blessed,
We've been under a Gothic shadow,
Now day breaks and points to the West.

In livery, once, in the name of
Some fiendish harmony,
The artist in Man lost the key to
His soul's own melody.

Its chorus floats over the Danube
In the citizen's free hullo,
In the new note of Haydn's 'London',
In the 'Marriage of Figaro'.

The Hero is in the Augarten
In the lover's sturm und drang,
It's spring on Napoleonstrasse
In the songs the soldiers sang.

In the thawed fields below Vienna
Where daffodils blow on the breeze,
The nobles who tie us hang withered
And Liberty's star fills the trees.

The birds fling their odes to freedom
In a Wienerwald symphony,
The sun streams in through my carriage
On a New Humanity.

(painting by Augustus Leopold Egg)

Nothing to do but doze. And I'm not
Soliciting the Artist's attentions, I'm just hot.
More stitched than Penelope's
Tapestry. The Gentlemen insist our
Destination is their little secret;
That we will love it. "The greater the number
Of trains, the greater the civilisation,"
Declares my Betrothed. But then he would,
His family owns the Line. Beatrice is lost
In the Death - not of Arthur, now - but Gordon,
Lives in her world of lost romance 'till Papa
Complains she'll tax him to death. He is so grim.
A married lady's Establishment to him
In a strong, slate-lidded box. To her it's
The Castle of the Lady of Shalott.
In spite of which, now I'm to change my hearth,
He says he'd die without her left to dream
Away his cares, his stocks and bonds and deeds
And doubts about his Final Destination.
Papa says Life's Journey really begins
And ends in the bosom of a loving family.
(Six of us departed at an early
Station - dear Mama in childbed - leaving
Little Albert still, and Dolly, and me
And Bea, my perfect image yet my opposite:
Don't fruit and flower share the same tree?)
The train is gathering more and more speed.
In the cabin next door the Gentlemen's voices
Appear to be raised. Will's in a frenzy
About our progress. My view's unchanged:
Unambitious hills and waves, an upright
Wood; a weak and gothically girded sky.
I sway, feel a flutter of doubt, but nod.

Steam's building up and up, up to a scream,
Bea's reading Morte - not of Gordon - but God.
Could I raise the alarm with propriety?
Or call for Papa, or Will? Or leave my place?
No. Better more tightly shut my eyes,
More fervently clasp my hands. And pray
The Picnic planned at Century's End
Is not getting further, and further, away.

I.
F.R.Reich, Dental Surgeon, S.S.A.,
Runes pressed in the cold
April blond plate outside,
Drilled in my child's memory.
Swallowed like blood, his earnest
Jokes of sweet-toothed frauleins.
But with us he was noted for kindness,
Treated me, thus, as a child
Right up to 'Thirty Six, when all ended.
JEWS TO LOSE VOTE in headlines, heels
Clipped together, he courteously 'regretted'
Our family could not in future be treated,
By him, as Germans. I ran
A dry tongue across the rotten ache,
Finding the gold he'd foot-drilled in
Four years before to my girl's empty head
- While I counted....in, in, in, out, out
The rings on the lamp overhead;
He in bright mood at Hindenberg's win,
His hand, and smiling political chit chat, made light
With *that Austrian's* drubbing.

II.
More rain - don't they ever get tired of it?
Sweat from Mexico
Distilled by this creeping
Cold from Europe, damping
My spirit. Light washing over
Stone steps before blackout
Brings no comfort; the railing licks
Cold my supported hand.
A dark, dumb terror articulated
Too many times, interned in files
Screaming with figures, birth dates, death dates,
'Family In Custody', 'deported', 'evicted',
'arrested',
Begins to be meaningless,
A little crazy - one of Father's
Hysterical jokes. Resistance,
Capitulation. And, at last, Escape,
All broken down in the shabby
Second-hand language of this race
Interned in a Crypt, peaceful Sundays
Smashed by the hideous wail of sirens, explosions,
Gun-bursts, pyred horizons.

III.
I came here in 'Thirty Eight, just before
The 'vengeance' pogrom.
Odd, but when the Nazis
Kicked in from the cold first
(The Elections in 'Thirty)
I thought *Jews* were just a
Vote-catching gimmick. The Storm Troops
Came out of the gutter
But their ideals sang: Germany the strong
Stirred heart of Europe, a nation
Which astounded West, and humiliated East
In the War made Great with that Valkyrie spirit
Our enemies failed to explain
Away as mere 'organisation'.
Father won the Iron Cross, the
Fatherland its world destiny:
One thousand million per cent
Inflation, then the four (five, six)
Unemployed millions; a Reichstag
Of Bolsheviks. Who cared, then, if a few Reds asked
For broken heads and got them?

IV.
The Elections of 'Twenty Four were wild. We
Saw the first Nazis
And we boycotted
Eve, the Communist's daughter.
Nothing seemed absolute
Then. Over in England
The first Workers' Government, at
Home sixty Reds, and no
Guns to keep out the Soviets,
Father said. I'm still afraid of how cruel
I felt and was, how exhilarated, though I was
Only ten, and yearning, perhaps, to be accepted.
Then the reversed Cross I'd watched
For my sixth birthday, when the Free Corps
Marched on union Berlin, brought
Back excitement again. Breathtaking, too,
The red & black swathe, armbands, boots.
I almost wished them to single me out
(Aren't Hitler and Freud from the same place?),
Conceived a brief crush on the eagle-eyed
schoolboy
Who drilled our local Jungvolk.

V.
Many friends, of our class, voted Nazi
Through the Depression.
Some, to better themselves
Or their chance of a job.
Joined them. But it was only
When *The Corporal* goosed in
To be Chancellor that the dream
- Unhealthy, adolescent -
Turned into the nightmare you can't repress.
We dodged the first persecutions,
Protected by Father's high rank in the Army.
(There were five hundred thousand others besides - then.)
Nationality was lost
By one or two - humiliating
And a real fright. Yet still we thought
Once Chancellor - President - Hitler got
Economy and unions
Under control, it would all blow
Over. But the unrest continued,
Came marching the streets, looking for us. New regulations
Each week; reduced to 'subjects'.

VI.
Our newspapers were stopped, but Otto spared
The new conscription:
Poor exchange for my loss
Of a second-year place
At the University;
Gretel couldn't wed Hans
Next: she was, they said, an 'Ayran'.
Our passports got harder
To get, and, with War in the air, I knew
It was time to uproot while we could.
Our Austrian relations soon weren't far enough,
Nor, then, Czechoslovakia. We managed it
On the 4th of October
1938, one day before
They marked the passports with a 'J'.
A (Nazi) friend in the office helped me,
Dropped the new 'Sarah' from my name,
Helga 'Sarah' Helbrow sounded
So oppressed, as 'Israel' Einstein would have,
The way 'Israel' Freud might have analysed
Goebbels' Vienna, newly Doctored.

VII.
'Stateless' (starving) Jews went first, to Poland,
I heard, land of slaves.
In Paris, I cheered as
The Nazi Attache
Was shot (by a Jew). Goebbels'
'Spontaneous' pogrom
Followed, all through the Reich. Even
In Paris, I feared it.
In its wake, financially crippling laws,
Curfews, closures, exclusions, spoils,
All goose-stepped up, and up, then marched into Poland
With yet more kick, declaring velt sturm, blitz krieg, War.
Last winter (Nineteen Forty),
I heard that Father, too proud to run,
Unpensioned, with unprotected
Rent, uncouponed, dispossessed, no
Radio, phone, 'reparations'
Unpaid, chose 'protective custody'.
I heard he went in a cattle truck.

VIII.
I never thought much about *Being A Jew*
'Till I found myself
Cowed, on a train screaming
Out of Berlin. Hidden
With our remnant of luggage
Was a Rabbi, Wanted
By The Gestapo. (My cousin's
Family are synagogue
Goers, Festival-observers: too other -
Worldy for me, and quite willing
To risk the whole exodus for this priest, although
Even Mother had got more orthodox by then.)
I listened while he intoned
The Chosen People's star role: to lead
The World from the Wilderness, to
Lead from Totem to Civilisation
In Art, Science, Finance, Song & Laughter.
In fidelity to God His
Foremost nation; in losing His Faith's Way
The scorn of slaves; our gift for survival, the true
badge Of David. And then they came.

IX.
Jews had to call themselves Unbelievers, those
Two hundred thousand
- And falling - left behind
For "The Final Solution".
But I remember the wailing
Along the corridor
When they took the Rabbi away,
Powerlust on their hate-
Cultured faces, eyes sharp as bunker bats;
I heard the voice of a people,
A great and greatly suffering people, wailing
All the way back to David, and Moses, wailing
All the way back to Jacob,
Abraham, wailing all the way back
To God. Sweating blood, I wailed too.
And it was breathtaking. Like coming home.
Emotion, doubtless. Not surprising
In the circumstances: my home
And whole life wheeling back towards
The darkened heart of Europe; Mozart's discipline shot.
One had to wail then. Or die.

X.
Mother naturally wants to forget
Germany, but, lately,
It seems, the West as well.
Since coming to England,
She's taken up Hebrew
Scripture and lore, though (as
They say, even here, even now,-
"You can't keep a Jew down")
Not yet so unworldy she couldn't get
Work for me in the bombed-out School.
It's hardly Goethe, but helps my English, and to
Build a future. A divine spirit of defiance
Moves these people, allied to
Their deep suspicion of foreigners:
Two little boys screeching JEW, JEW
In my class today, like hardened Nazis,
Shook me as much as that thousand
Pounder cratered in the Churchyard,
Tombstones, decay, rubbled through windows.
Nationhood, race - all the past - is dead. Only
God is now worth fighting for.

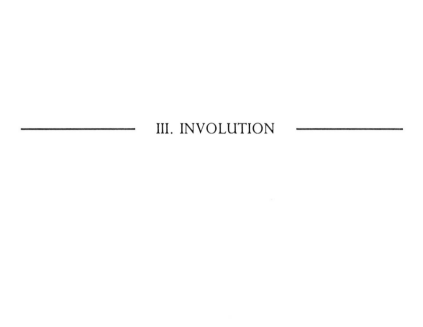

III. INVOLUTION

'Involution' is a progressive sequence about human striving for perfection, happiness, freedom, truth or whatever one chooses to call it. The religions call it God but in practice almost always ignore it in favour of dogma, conformity or ritual, or war against someone else's dogma, conformity or ritual. The writing is a different, highly experimental, kind from 'Evolution' and 'Ghosts' exploring a formal intensity perhaps unusual in modern poetry. Both form and content are speculative adaptations of the Urdu 'ghazal', a highly wrought and disciplined Indian love poem which it can take a poet a lifetime to master. Urdu ghazals are meant to be sung to Indian musical accompaniment and both words and music express intense longing for a beloved. (Heard on an Indian hillside at evening somewhere, their wailing cry from the heart can be hypnotically beautiful and affecting). Without the music, they retain an independent life as works of the highest literary merit, which is less generally true of Western song lyrics.

Ghazals originate from the Sufi mystics of classical Persia, whose extravagant Zoroastrian-influenced metaphors of lovemaking and intoxication got them into the same kind of trouble with orthodox Islam as gnostic Christians got into with the Church. The nearest Western equivalents, if there are any, are the Italian sonnet, said to derive at the Renaissance in both form and spirit from this Arab ghazal and, more remotely, the Song of Solomon, with its synthesis of romantic passion and mystical intent. Each couplet in a ghazal must be self-sufficient, a poem in itself, only linked to the rest by the demanding metrical pattern (believed to synergise mind with heart forces), peculiar rhyme scheme, and by the prevailing mood of love and complaint. The convention that the poet addresses himself in the final couplet is adapted in these poems to a persona identifying himself there by name. In the last seven ghazals, this persona, representative in each case of the degree of love expressed, identifies *herself*. There is a tradition in Eastern and Western devotional literature -outside of Islam- of such passion being female. Though trivialised and exploited, it is a tradition of immense force and I have kept to it.

In Involution the evolutionary process towards the highest pitch of self-interest is reversed; the process is rather towards total self-surrender. The gathering motive force of Evolution (at work also in 'Ghosts') was the instinct for self-preservation and survival perfected in the most successful species, the human. The gathering motive force of Involution, on the contrary, is love. The sequence speculates that as human love intensifies and increases in maturity, it precipitates higher and higher planes of consciousness which are less and less self-obscured and survival-centred, less and less materially based, more and more 'divine' in the Blakean sense. These planes are thus increasingly remote from ordinary human reality (in terms of such reality they are madness) and nearer and nearer to reality as experienced by the lover or mystic. However, the everyday alienation most of us experience as a vague uneasiness is, to such a lover/mystic, agony, because the ecstasy of fulfilment - what they, like we, are missing - is all the more clearly identified, but still not possessed. We see it through a glass darkly: they see it - blissfully yet desperately - face to face. In ordinary human love, the beloved is experienced as being both outside oneself and at the same time as essential to one's being. The result is a kind of blissful anguish. This same experience, in the ghazals of Hafiz for example, is described as intensifying further through no less than seven broadly identifiable stages, each a deeper and more powerful love than the last. These stages precipitate in turn seven broadly identifiable planes of consciousness, each a more complete realisation of human potential than the former. In the Christian myth of Lucifer's fall, love (for God) loses at the last its titanic struggle with a separate self-interest. In Hafiz the long struggle is actually won. Its consummation is the final annihilation of a sense of self as separate from the beloved (described elsewhere, by Buddha, as Nirvana).

Attempting to describe these stages in ghazal form became rather like writing archetypes or myths *where myth is understood as being more, not less, real than everyday life*. The last seven ghazals suggest broadly different kinds of human love - romantic, matrimonial, maternal, passionate, devotional, bereaved, 'reunited'. They have an independent literal meaning. But the sequence as such traces a transcendental progression - a growing out of self - inherent in all love.

Muse, give Hiroshima's Homer and Dante (the world's nations
Drone in my throat like a chorus of swans) inspiration.

Grilled by your interview council, of chic neo-Muses, I'm
Struck by your hands with their lovelier waves of oration.

'Who?, who are you?' says your forefinger. "Nothing,without loving
You.   All I've done's what I am, my continued creation."

Clio asks "Name?".   I can see it engraved, all it stood for, in
Immortal places....But art is in self's uncreation.

"Show us your route map," Euterpe interprets, "of Love's ascent
In to the lover, through heartland's unveiled desolation."

"I am the Ocean of Love," you declare, to this broken but
Unbursting bubble of dream, "I have come to awaken."

Muser, as platforms are churned into bubbles, by easterly
Rain, "Find Nirvana from Fenland," resounds through the station.

How can love's spiel be heard here?

After Auchswitz, what heart lyrical?
After the hell of a loveless day, what desk top and quill?

Yours a love feast past all dreaming of,
Wine by the Ocean and welcome, ah, but who'll pay the bill?

Through the barbed wire, your smile radiates,
Making my thorniest garland thrive; your bloom makes me ill.

Our affair's hopeless. Stop asking a
Man to start dying of love whom all his life's trained to kill.

Answer, "Heart speech is love's melody.
Tune in, my rhythm'll break yours free as no other will."

Yours an old wine of such subtlety,
Just to refuse it's a joy, against the full force of will.

Love's the sole song - so stop wandering,
Judah, away from the foot; get started up Lovers' Hill.

Chasing a love that refuses to die

Born to escape me, all over the world, in a million
Different lives, and that 'I' - seeking you's - still unshaken.

"Faith in our love would sow faith in your self, sowing faith in this
Life made of failings and fears," you say. Ah, I don't listen.

Losing rememberance of you, I have haunted the phantoms I
Killed myself fleeing, in houses of lost incarnation.

Passing through female and male for your love, I revive every
Heartbeat that's passed in my soul, every joy and frustration.

Follow your question? I can't. And the answer? (I love you so)
Lost in a million lifeworks achieved; in gestation.

Drag your sore eyes from the Westering sun you fool: love's dawning
Burns out of history, which East dreams as reincarnation.

Dreamer, why trouble your head about how to proceed with this?
Follow your heart, through the sighs of its long consummation.

The divinest new teacher has come to our school.
In a swirling of stars, I eclipse every rule.

As his brilliant dark look unblinds my mind's eye
To his heart-piercing question, I glow like a fool.

I am deaf to the end of his first lesson bell.
All the bells in my heart keep me fixed to the stool.

I must hand him my pages of error and shame
With the angels a choir in my ears, high and cool.

Though you're dazed by my radiance: striking its chord
Is his voice, humming, "Love is the key to it all".

To just drift through these corridors - echoing, bright -
Where his presence has lingered, is blissful, is cruel.

O Blue Stocking, your long insight's lost in this dream
- But his beam can cut straight to your heart, like a jewel.

Through a thousand years I've loved him more and more,
Now his fresh white rose is all I'm breathing for.

On a breathless trail, my nose for grossness lost
In these blazing scents, I burn to reach his core.

Just to think of him unlocks our love's perfume,
Makes the pure light clear and tunes me to the score.

Now the dried-up churchyard tree shall spring to life.
"This is love," he beams, "which nothing can ignore."

All the power from his ring I hold in hand,
Through the fine torn veil my eyes are burned the more.

Novice, feed this pealing kiss, this heaven-fire,
And let Now's fine essence linger, ever more.

I'm a goddess! but my wild love must come back down to the Earth
Just to skivvy for his fixed will, just to suffer a rebirth.

He's my heart's child and I worship every gesture that he makes.
Must I share him with the whole world? Is it tortured with his dearth?

As his cord tugs to that harsh world, makes my heart sore with his cry,
All my wishes free as lightning, wafts of ambrose, know his girth.

From Olympus, love must wing down, past a harp chord in a cloud
Of some cheap scent, past a dream land, to this child's play, to have worth.

O Earthed Angel, all your blown heart's sweet enchantment he'll dispel
Crying, "True love can't be forcefed. It's the breast milk of the Earth."

Mortal blitzkrieg's a mere shadow of my splendour, but above
- More than Pure Will's look of thunder, lash of lightning, - is our love.

When he kissed me, I was Yezdan, I was Allah, as the moth
Who in power and in glory beats the flood-flames of her love.

"Do not once," warned my beloved, "try to conquer other selves.
If you conquer yours, you've conquered there the whole world in my love."

In a dark night he has left me crying blindly for his glare:
Turn the hell-scorch of this longing to the blazed pain of your love!

In your agony, bright Lucy, you could smash worlds into dust.
All your star mind is exploding, in the space void of his love.

In a far land where my thoughts throng by like strangers, I'm at home;
Every dirt track, every silk step over marble, is his own.

There are twinned queues for his rich port, endless pulped forms left to fi
Lovers' thin bribes, like the beggared, seek a short cut to his dome.

Through his doorway, I'm delivered from a rickshaw driven blind
Through the headlights, in his still room, I can think through where he's flow

All unravelled in his presence, all the heavens in a thought;
I am sight-drunk on the soul-bliss of the vision he has shown.

All this heartland made of cracked crags, which his slaves heave up the hill
Every thought-bloom, all this sunlight in my mind's Eye, he has sown.

Were he Lord Ram, though his blood-foe, for his Sita I would die:
Were he Albert, as his Sita, in a grave dress I would moan.

O Miss Know All, distant Empress of the thought world, hear his song:
"Do not seek, child; it's your own veil, like a cobweb, must be blown!"

Om is a sound used in Indian meditation

Seeing is believing: glimpsed in youth this Love-sick Mazdah;
Seen, now, dancing slim and strong at dawn in shining sadra.

Everywhere in everything and endlessly I see him
Face to childlike mirrored face who calls me now his Radha.

No desire or energy or thought or trial exists now.
Only his in whom I feel and breathe and am my Master.

Archangelic heart-to-hearts, his hands as quick as feeling,
Close my eyes to slower worlds: his larks lift spirit's purdah.

Manhood wrecked with fasts and burdens, sacrifice and service,
Pangs of separation (borrowed): God could work no harder.

Skyward-staring, fractured-limbed, in agony, he's calling,
"Help my darling first", the purest feeling, mind's unmasker.

Eye to eye now, reading "One not we", his feet I'm pressing.
Cuttings, curls, his silenced seed of withered joys, I garner.

O Marie, this lonely grief, these flames of lover's longing
Finely veil you. And your opened Eye's the one outsider.

sadra: a long white muslin robe.
Radha: Krishna's divine counterpart or bride

This is God.   On the highest of highs through the gulf of a tomb,
(This is God), I'm on top of the worlds born of mind, spirit, womb.

I am not.   Now the bubble has burst, there is nothing but sea:
This is God.   I'm as drowned in his kiss as the bud in her bloom.

I'm in Love.   All the pain in my heart's disappeared like a dream:
This is God.   I am dead to the worlds yet awake to my swoon.

I am him.   Now the primal beloved and lover are one:
This is God.   I've become who I journeyed towards and from whom.

O my love!   He's embraced me and brought me at last to himself:
This is God.   Now I see there is only my Self in the room.

I'm the soul.   "There's no dark where there's light, no unknown where
one knows."
This is God.   Little mind has been razed with its search and its gloom.

O my Self!   You're beyond the beyond but you're found on the Earth.
This is God - All in All - in the flesh: its perfection, and tomb.